Applications of Power Electronics

Reza Talee

First Edition

Copyrights © 2021

All Rights Reserved for the Author; Reza Talee.

Published by American Academic Research, USA

No part of this book may be reprinted or reproduced utilized in any electronic, mechanical or other means now known or here after invented, including photocopying and recording or any information storage or retrieval system, without permission in writing from the authors.

Title: Applications of Power Electronics
Author: Reza Talee
ISBN: 978-1947464261
Publisher: American Academic Research, USA

Table of Contents

- INTRODUCTION 5
- Overcurrent 10
- Applications of Power Electronic Devices 10
- Semi-Conductor Devices 11
- Wide Band gap Materials 11
- Power Electronics in Industries 11
- Power Electronics Industry Analysis 12
- Market 13
- Technology 13
- Suppliers 14
- New Applications 14
- Power Electronic Devices That Act as Solid-State Switches 15
- Power Diodes 15
- To know it quantitatively, able to utilize the S – factor. Ratio T_b/T_a: Delicateness figure or S-factor. S-factor: degree of the voltage transitory that happens amid the time the diode recoups. S-f 20
- Schottky Diode 20
- Metal-Oxide Semiconductor Field-Effect Transistor (MOSFET) 21
- Power Bipolar Junction Transistor (BJT) 34
- Insulated-Gate Bipolar Transistor (IGBT) 39
- THYRISTORs (SCR, GTO, MCT) 44
- SCR 45
- GTO (Gate Turn-off THYRISTOR) 50
- MCT (MOS-Controlled THYRISTOR) 53
- References 57

INTRODUCTION

The first hardware insurgency started in 1948 with the development of the silicon transistor was proposed by Chime Labs and commercially delivered by Common Electric within the prior fifties. Mercury Bend Rectifiers were well in utilize by that time and the strong and compact. In power electronics SCR was the primary begun supplanting it within the rectifiers and cyclo-converters. The moment gadgets transformation started with the improvement of a commercial THYRISTOR by the Common Electric Company in 1958 and was the starting of an unused period of control gadgets. Since at that point, numerous diverse sorts of control semiconductor gadgets and change strategies have been introduced.

By and large, control gadgets are the method of utilizing semiconductor exchanging gadgets to control and change over electrical control stream from one frame to another to meet a particular require. In other words, control gadgets empower the control of the control stream as well as its frame ac or dc and the greatness of streams and voltages. Having the foremost progressed innovation for control electronic gadgets, silicon (Si) control gadgets can be handled with essentially no fabric deformity. Be that as it may, silicon innovation has a few impediments for higher control utility applications. The essential restriction of Si gadgets is voltage blocking capacity due to the limit band crevice (1.1eV), which limits the voltage blocking capacity to less than to 10kv. For higher voltage applications, stacking bundled gadgets in arrangement is required. Stacking bundle is sweeping from a pressing point of view.

Thus, there are motivating forces to create gadgets having awesome voltage blocking capacity in a same or littler device package. Such gadgets can be utilized in an assortment of utility exchanging applications from dissemination level (tens of kV) to transmission levels (>100kv).

Amid the final two decades, there has been a huge increment within utilization of control electronic gadgets and are able of performing different capacities such as amendment, amplification, control and era. Within the therapeutic field, a few of the therapeutic gadgets make utilize of gadgets and ECG (electrocardiograph) utilized to discover the condition of the heart of the quiet, EEG (electroencephalograph) utilized for recording the electrical movement of the brain, EMG (electromyography) utilized for deciding the movement of the muscles, X-ray machine used for taking pictures of inside bone structure conjointly for treatment of a few infections.

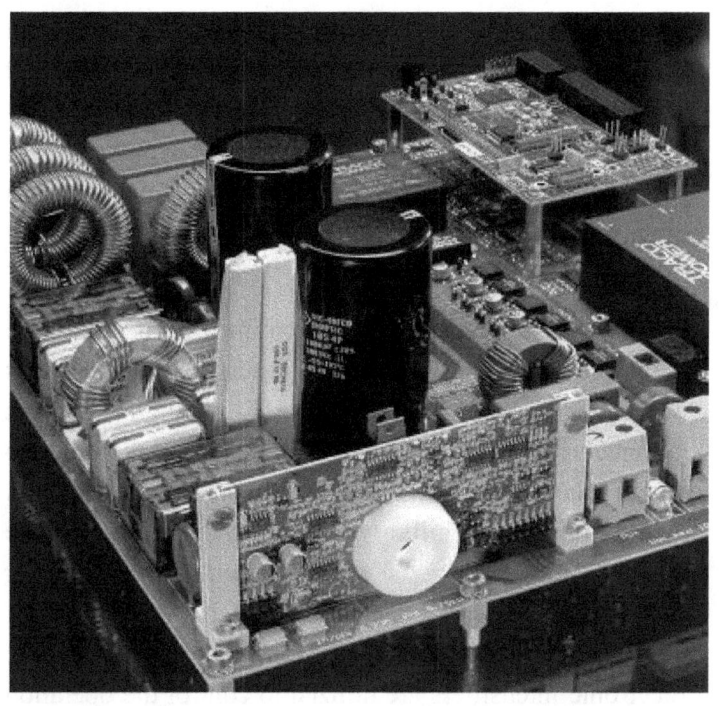

Electronic circuits are utilized for controlling numerous operations such as control of thickness of a work, dampness substance in a material for fast arithmetical calculations electronic computers are utilized for programmed record keeping and fathoming of complicated issues. Any computer can be associated to web through an electronic gadget, called the modem. Electronic connect is being utilized to transmit and get email and fax messages. Use of programmed control framework in industry is expanded day by day. Speed of mechanical engines is controlled through THYRATRONS, THYRISTORs or attractive amplifiers.

Instrumented plays an imperative part in any industry and inquire about organization for exact estimation of different amounts. Precision of hardware rebellious such as cathode-ray oscilloscope, strain gages, recurrence counter etc. is much higher than that of conventional disobedient. No inquire about research facility is completed without reasonable electronic disobedient.

Discuss activity is controlled electronically. It is through the RADAR (Radio Location and Extending) that nation is watched from foe flying machine. By utilizing RADAR, it is conceivable not as it were to distinguish, but moreover to decide the precise area and speed of the adversary air ship. Most of the modern military assault and discovery gear are worked electronically. Electronic circuits are utilized for controlling numerous operations such as control of thickness of a work, dampness substance in a fabric. Electronic intensifiers are utilized to control the operation of programmed door-openers, lightning frameworks, sound frameworks, control frameworks and security devices. Control hardware can be found in control framework in numerous shapes inside the control framework. These shapes extend from tall voltage coordinate current (HVDC) converter station to an adaptable ac transmission framework (Realities) gadgets that are utilized to control and control ac control lattices, variable speed drives for engines, the electric drive in transportation frameworks, blame current restricting gadgets, the solid-state dispersion transformer, and exchange switches. The challenge confronting the control framework building nowadays is to utilize existing transmission offices to a more noteworthy impact. Progressing utilization of the existing control frameworks is given through the application of progressed control advances in control hardware based gear or Actualities. Truths give demonstrated specialized arrangements to address unused working challenges being displayed nowadays. With that said, Realities are as well costly to buy, introduce, and keep up within the current utility frameworks.

Contrasts in fundamental highlights of gadgets call for extraordinary assurance plans specific for those devices. Power hardware can give utilities the capacity to more successfully conveying control to their customers whereas giving expanded unwavering quality to the bulk control framework. Control hardware can moreover play a significant part in making strides security of the nation's electric lattice. In spite of the fact that it is exceptionally troublesome to evaluate unwavering quality benefits, thinks about appear the assessed display esteem of amassed qualities of solid, modernized lattice to be USD 638 to USD 802 billion over a twenty-year skyline, with annualized values of between USD 51 and USD 64 billion/year. With that control gadgets aren't considered perfect frameworks. A few of the imperative issues the control gadgets experience incorporate taken a toll, unwavering quality, cooling strategies, productivity, warm administration and control. Power electronic converters frequently work from the utility mains and are uncovered to the unsettling influences related with it.

Overcurrent
di/dt.

Voltage spikes or over-voltages.

Gate-under voltage. Over voltage at gate. Excessive temperature rise.

Electro-static discharge.

A few of these strategies are common for all gadgets and converters. In any case, contrasts in basic highlights of gadgets call for extraordinary security plans specific for those devices.

Applications of Power Electronic Devices

Tall proficiency due to moo misfortune in control semiconductor devices.

- Tall unwavering quality of control electronic converter systems.
- Long life and less upkeep due to the nonappearance of any moving parts.
- Quick energetic reaction of the control electronic systems.
- Little measure and less weight result in less floor space and lower establishment cost.
- Mass generation of control semiconductor gadgets has brought about in lower taken a toll of the converter equipment.

Semi-Conductor Devices

Create high-voltage, high-current SiC gadgets for utility applications. • Create low-cost SiC IGBT gadgets to raise the capability of control gadgets in utility applications by supplanting GTOs.

Wide Band gap Materials

Conduct system-level affect considers to assess the effect of wide bandgap semiconductors on the utility grid. Develop high temperature pressing to require advantage of the capability of SiC devices. Develop inventive wide bandgap materials forms to make moo taken a toll, deformity free wafers.

Power Electronics in Industries

The prospect of control hardware designing created an assortment of device which are utilized within the way of life of mankind. Utilizing novel properties of hardware, the researchers are making an unused imaginative fabric. The later progress is that the gadget which ponder the light waves may offer assistance to open up the electromagnetic run by terahertz. Terahertz innovation is already developed to petahertz innovation to consider the unmistakable light. Control Hardware could be a chief producer of Tall Recurrence Inverters and Insides Roof Lighting Arrangements for Transport and Coach Industry and authorized merchant of Driven Goal Show Signs from a driving European producer, M/s Hanover Shows Ltd. UK for the complete Indian subcontinent. We too bargain in activity administration framework, stopping administration framework and ticket distributing machine. Control Hardware is the innovation related with effective change, control and conditioning of electric control from its accessible input into the required electrical

Power Electronics Industry Analysis

Control gadgets control electric control at a wide run of voltages and streams, and the gadgets have applications in an assortment of expanded ranges. Modern innovations guarantee lower costs and higher proficiency, whereas producers investigate unused markets within the natural segment. Conceivable section focuses for small businesses exist within the get together of controlled control supplies within the moo control ranges.

Market

Advertise estimate gauges for the control gadgets industry extend from $20 billion for semiconductor gadgets as it were, to $70 billion in case control supplies built around control semiconductors are included. Clients are found in all major mechanical exercises, wherever electric control must be controlled, and in sun powered control, wind control, electric cars, keen lattices, and aviation and shopper hardware. The bigger showcase incorporates companies that utilize control semiconductors in amassing control electronic frameworks to supply loads such as computers, Televisions, engines and chemical forms.

Technology

Control semiconductors can be exchanged from a protection to a conducting condition by the application of a control current or voltage. This characteristic permits you to embed the semiconductor gadget into an electric circuit and switch the control on and off exceptionally rapidly, controlling the sum of control that's conveyed to a stack. Verifiably, the semiconductor fabric has been silicon, but more current gadgets based on gallium nitride and silicon carbide are in improvement and guarantee higher execution at lower taken a toll. In most applications, the control semiconductors are coordinates into a control supply with extra components for control and for coordinating the inputs and yields to the electrical supply and the stack.

Suppliers

Providers of control semiconductors incorporate most major hardware producers in North America, Europe and Asia. In expansion to providing control gadgets to producers of control supplies, numerous of these companies moreover create huge control supply modules for utilize in applications such as electric networks, wind control and electric cars. The advertise for littler control modules, such as for computers, battery chargers and sun powered cells, is served by both universal providers and littler, nearby companies that specialize in specific applications. The neighborhood providers frequently deliver custom-designed control hardware for particular clients.

New Applications

The control gadgets advertise is developing since modern applications are supplementing a consistent request from conventional mechanical companies. The developing segments incorporate control gadgets utilized in wind turbines to coordinate the variable control created by the turbine generator to the network; little inverters utilized for sun based boards to alter coordinate current into rotating current for lattice and family utilize; control gadgets for electric vehicles to control the electric control from the batteries; and keen network applications that permit utilities to control streams. Little producers can discover specialty markets in these modern areas, particularly within the little wind turbine and sun powered vitality markets.

Power Electronic Devices That Act as Solid-State Switches

This specialized article is devoted to the audit of the taking after control electronic gadgets which act as solid-state switches within the circuits. They act as a switch without any mechanical movement. Power Diodes Metal-Oxide-Semiconductor Field-Effect Transistor (MOSFET) Bipolar -Intersection Transistor (BJT) Insulated-Gate Bipolar Transistor (IGBT) THYRISTORs (SCR, GTO, MCT) Solid-state gadgets are totally made from a strong fabric and their stream of charges is kept inside this strong fabric. This title "solid state" is regularly utilized to appear a contrast with the prior advances of vacuum and gas-discharge tube gadgets; conjointly to prohibit the routine electro-mechanical gadgets (transfers, switches, difficult drives and other gadgets with moving parts). The transistor by Chime Labs in 1947 was the primary solid-state gadget to come into commercial utilize afterward within the 1960s. In this article, comparative solid-state gadgets such as control diode, control transistor, MOSFET, THYRISTOR and its Two-Tran.

Power Diodes

A control diode features a P-I-N structure as compared to the flag diode having a P-N structure. Here, I (in P-I-N) stands for inborn semiconductor layer to bear the high-level switch voltage as compared to the flag diode (n- float locale layer appeared in Fig. 2). Be that as it may, the disadvantage of this inborn layer is that it includes recognizable resistance amid forward-biased condition. Hence, control diode requires an appropriate cooling course of action for taking care of huge control dissemination. Control diodes are utilized in various applications counting rectifier, voltage clamper, voltage multiplier and etc. Control diode image is the same as of the flag diode as appeared in Fig.1.

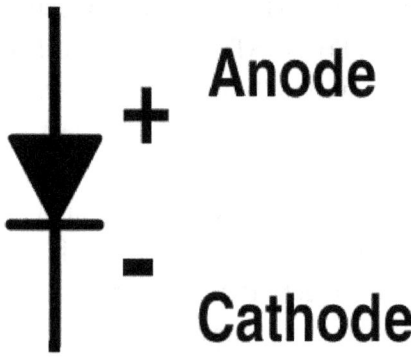

Figure 1. Symbol for Power Diode

Other highlights that are joined within the control diode letting it handle bigger control are: (a) Utilize of protect rings (b) Coating of Silicon Dioxide Layer Guard rings are of p-type that avoids their consumption layer consolidate with the exhaustion layer of the reverse-biased P-N intersection

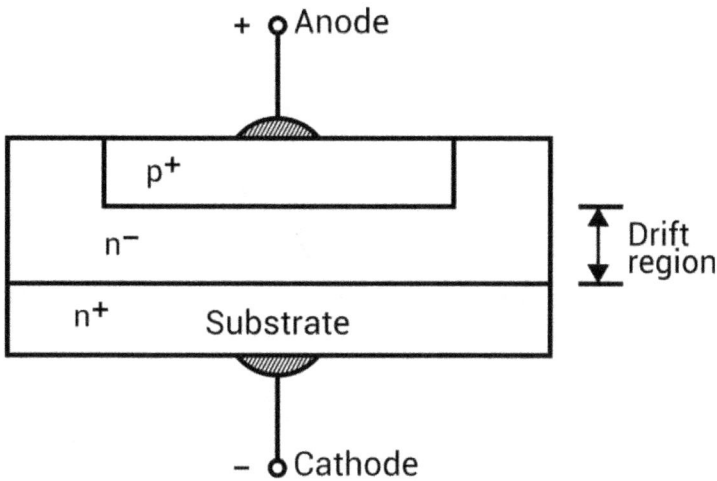

Figure 2. Structure of Power Diode

. The watch rings anticipate the sweep of the ebb and flow of the consumption layer boundary to gotten to be as well limit which increments the breakdown quality. Coating of SiO2 layer makes a difference in restricting the electric field at the surface of the control diode. If thickness of gently doped I layer (n- layer) > exhaustion layer width at breakdown ⇒ Non-punch through control diode. (This implies exhaustion layer has not punched through the lightly-doped n-layer.) If thickness of I layer < exhaustion layer width at breakdown ⇒ Punch through control diode. Characteristics of Control Diode the two sorts of characteristics of a control diode are appeared in Fig. 3 and Fig. 4 named as follows: (i) Amp-volt characteristics (i-v characteristics) (ii)

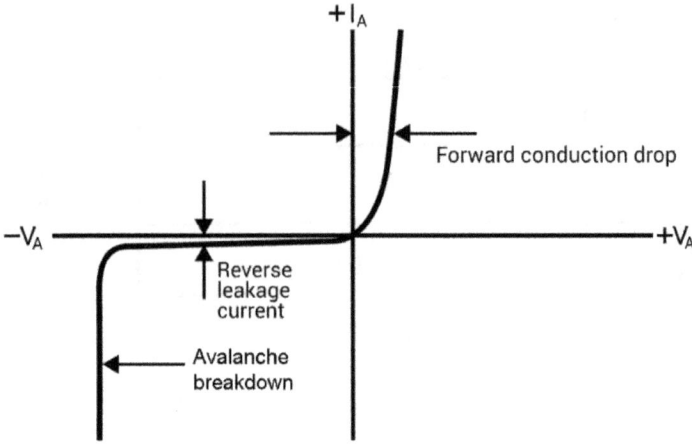

Figure 3. Amp-Volt Characteristics of Power Diode

Cut-in voltage is the esteem of the least voltage for VA (anode voltage) to form the diode works in forward conducting mode. Cut-in voltage of flag diode is 0.7 V whereas in control diode it is 1 V. So, its ordinary forward conduction drop is bigger. Beneath forward-bias condition, signal diode current increments exponentially and after that increment straightly. Within the case of the control diode, it nearly increments directly with the connected voltage as all the layers of P-I-N stay immersed with minority carriers beneath forward predisposition.

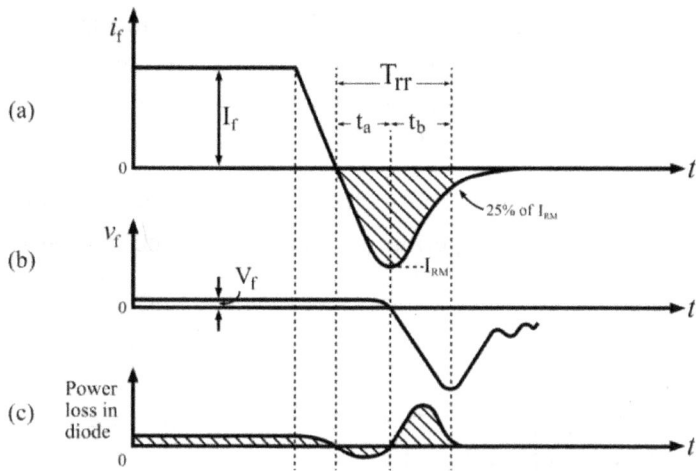

Figure 4. Turn-Off Characteristics of Power Diode: a) Variation of Forward Current if; b) Variation of Forward Voltage Drop v_f; c) Variation of Power Loss

Hence, a tall esteem of current produces comes about in voltage drop which cover the exponential portion of the bend. In reverse-bias condition, little spillage current streams due to minority carriers until the torrential slide breakdown shows up as appeared in Fig. 3. After the forward diode comes to invalid, the diode proceeds to conduct within the inverse heading since of the presence of put away charges within the exhaustion layer and the p or n-layer. The diode current streams for a reverse-recovery time t_{rr}. It is the time between the moment forward diode current gets to be zero and the moment reverse-recovery current rots to 25 % of its reverse greatest value. Time T_a: Charges put away within the consumption layer removed. Time T_b: Charges from the semiconductor layer is removed. Shaded zone in Fig 4.a speaks to put away charges QR which must be expelled amid reverse-recovery time t_{rr}. Power misfortune over diode = V_f * in the event that (appeared in Fig. 4.c)

As appeared, major control misfortune within the diode happens amid the period t_b. Recovery can be sudden or smooth as appeared in Fig. 5.

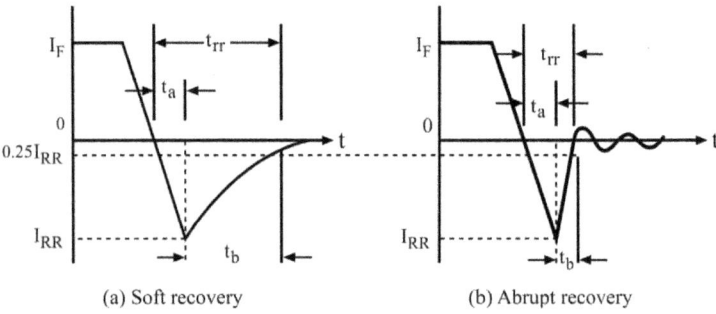

(a) Soft recovery (b) Abrupt recovery

Figure 5. Reverse-Recovery Characteristics for Power Diode

To know it quantitatively, able to utilize the S – factor. Ratio T_b/T_a: Delicateness figure or S-factor. S-factor: degree of the voltage transitory that happens amid the time the diode recoups. S-f

Schottky Diode

It has an aluminum-silicon intersection where the silicon is an n-type. As the metal has no gaps, there's no put away charge and no reverse-recovery time. Subsequently, there's as it was the development of the lion's share carriers (electrons) and the turn-off delay caused by recombination handle is maintained a strategic distance from. It can moreover switch off much speedier than a p-n intersection diode. As compared to the p-n intersection diode it has: (a) Lower cut-in voltage (b) Higher turn around spillage current (c) Higher working frequency Application: high-frequency instrumented and exchanging control supplies.

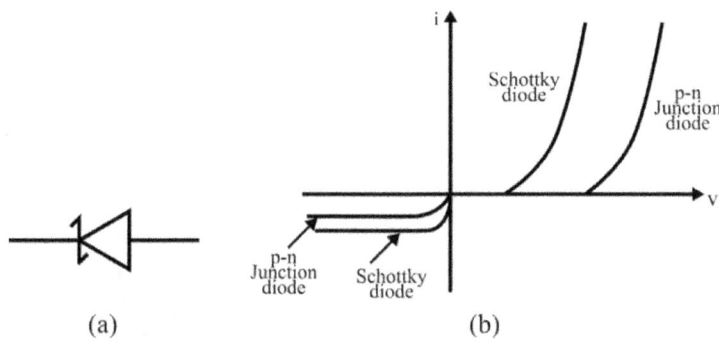

Figure 6. Schottky Diode Symbol and Current-Voltage Characteristics Curve

Metal-Oxide Semiconductor Field-Effect Transistor (MOSFET)

MOSFET could be a voltage-controlled lion's share carrier (or unipolar) three-terminal gadget. Its images are appeared in Fig. 7 and Fig. 8. As compared to the straightforward sidelong channel MOSFET for low-power signals, power MOSFET has diverse structure. It features a vertical channel structure where the source and the depletion layer are on the inverse side of the silicon wafer as appeared in Fig. 10. This inverse arrangement of the source and the deplete increments the capability of the control MOSFET to handle bigger control.

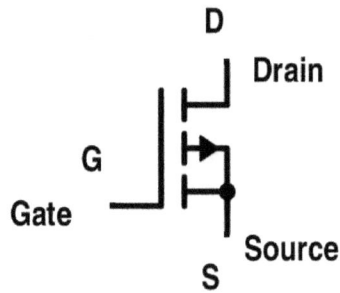

Figure 7. MOSFET Symbol

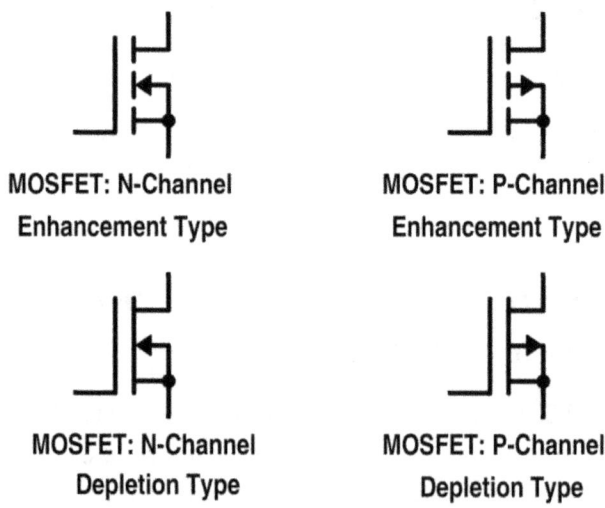

Figure 8. MOSFET Symbols for Different Modes

In all of these associations, substrates are inside associated. But in cases where it is associated remotely, the image will alter as appeared within the n-channel upgrade sort MOSFET in Fig. 9. N-channel upgrade sort MOSFET is more common due to tall versatility of electrons.

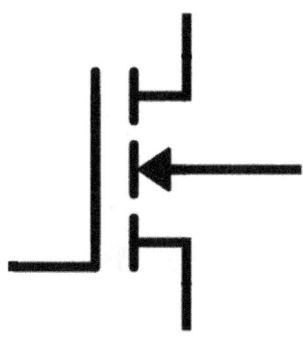

Figure 9. N-channel Enhancement-Type MOSFET with Substrate Connected Externally

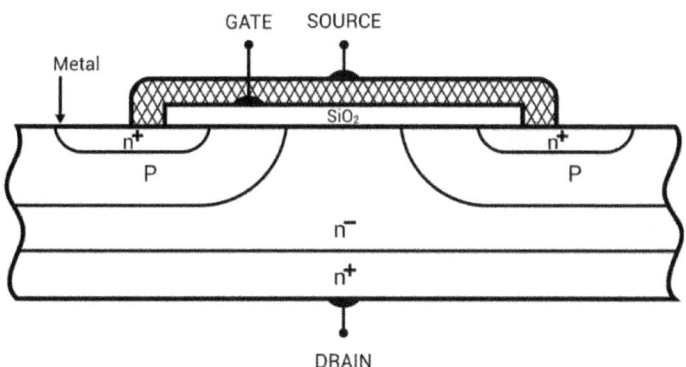

Figure 10. Cross-Sectional View of the Power MOSFET

Essential circuit chart and yield characteristics of an n-channel improvement control MOSFET with stack associated are in Fig. 11 and Fig. 12 individually.

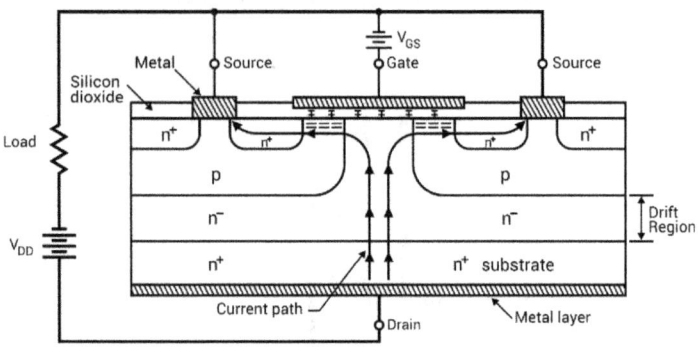

Figure 11. Power MOSFET Structural View with Connections

Drift locale appeared in Fig. 11 decides the voltage-blocking capability of the MOSFET. When $V_{GS} = 0$, $\Rightarrow V_{DD}$ makes it turn around one-sided and no current streams from deplete to source. When $V_{GS} > 0$, $\Rightarrow$ Electrons frame the current way as appeared in Fig. 11. Hence, current from the depletion layer to the source streams. Presently, in case we are going increment the gate-to-source voltage, deplete current will moreover increase.

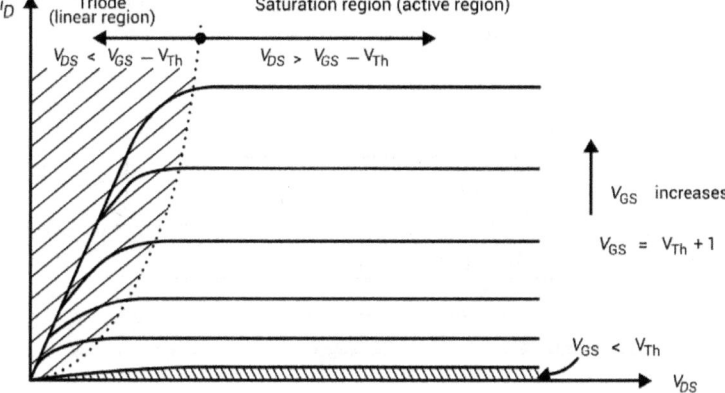

Figure 12. Drain Current (I_D) vs Drain-to-Source Voltage (V_{DS}) Characteristics Curves

For lower esteem of V_{DS}, MOSFET works in a direct locale where it encompasses a steady resistance rise to V_{DS} / I_D. For a settled esteem of V_{GS} and more noteworthy than edge voltage V_{TH}, MOSFET enters an immersion region where the esteem of the depletion layer current features a settled value.

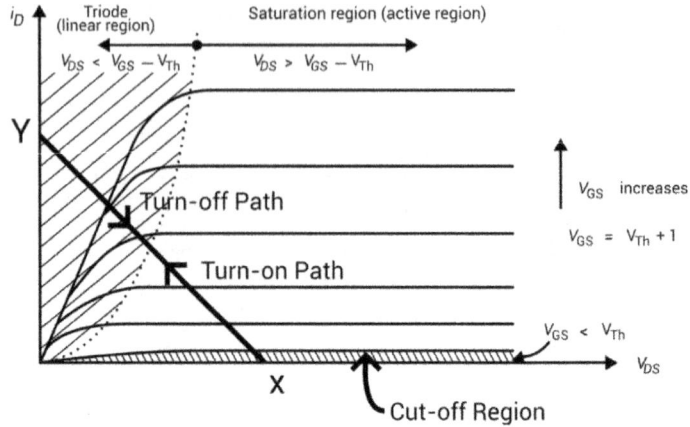

Figure 13. Output Characteristics with Load Line

In the event that XY speaks to the stack line, at that point the X-point speaks to the turn-off point and Y-point is the turn-on point where V_{DS} = (as voltage over the closed switch is zero). The heading of turning on and turning off prepare is additionally appeared in Fig. 13. Besides the yield characteristics bends, exchange characteristics of control MOSFET is additionally appeared in Fig. 14.

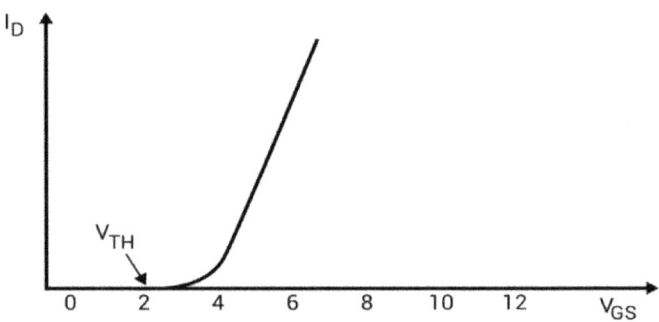

Figure 14. Gate-to-Source Voltage vs. Drain Current Characteristics for Power MOSFET

Here, V_{TH} is the least positive voltage between door and the source over which MOSFET comes in on-state from the off-state. This is often called threshold voltage. It is additionally appeared within the yield characteristics bend in Fig. 12. Close see of the auxiliary graph given in Fig. 11 uncovers that there exists an invented BJT and an imaginary diode structure implanted within the control MOSFET as appeared in Fig. 15. As source is connected to both base and emitter of this parasitic BJT, emitter and base of the BJT are brief circuited. Meaning this BJT acts in cut-off state.

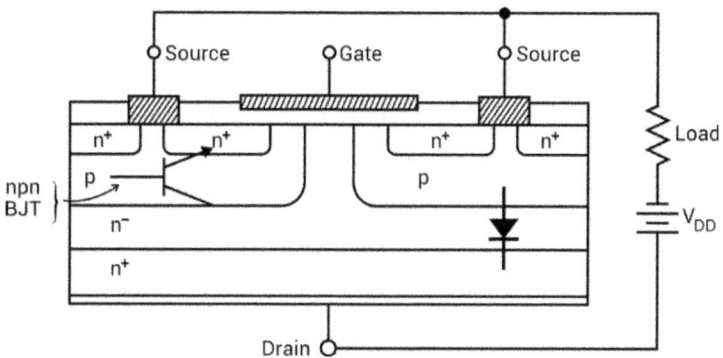

Figure 15. Fictitious BJT and Fictitious Diode in the Power MOSFET

Imaginary diode anode is associated to the source and its cathode is associated to the depletion layer. So, in case we apply the negative voltage V_{DD} over the depletion layer and source, it'll be forward one-sided. Meaning, the reverse-blocking capability of the MOSFET breaks. Hence, this could be utilized in inverter circuit for receptive loads without the requirement of intemperate diode over a switch. Typically, it is spoken to in Fig. 16.

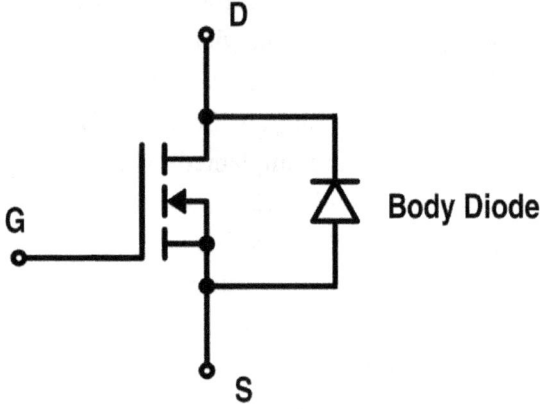

Figure 16. MOSFET Representation with Internal Body Diode

In spite of the fact that MOSFET inner body diode has adequate current and exchanging speed for most of the applications, there may be a few applications where the utilize of ultra-fast diodes is required. In such cases, an outside fast-recovery diode is associated in an antiparallel way. But a slow-recovery diode is additionally required to piece the body diode activity as given in Fig. 17.

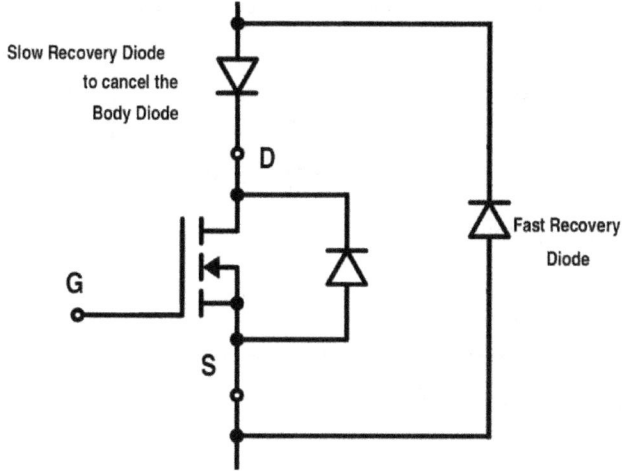

Figure 17. Implementation of Fast-Recovery Diode for Power MOSFET

One of the vital parameters that influences the exchanging characteristics is the body capacitances existing between its three terminals i.e. deplete, source and door. Its representation is appeared in Fig. 18.

Parameters C_{GS}, C_{GD} and C_{DS} are all non-linear in nature and given within the device's information sheet of a specific MOSFET. They moreover depend on the DC inclination voltage and the device's structure or geometry.

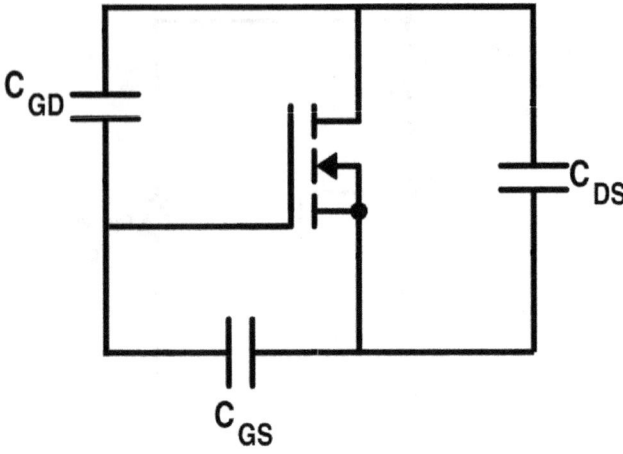

Figure 18. MOSFET Representation Showing Junction Capacitances

They must be charged through door amid turn-on handle to really turn on the MOSFET. The drive must be competent of charging and releasing these capacitances to switch on or switch off the MOSFET. Thus, the exchanging characteristics of a control MOSFET depend on these inner capacitances and the inside impedance of the entryway drive circuits. Too, it depends on the delay due to the carrier transport through the float locale. Exchanging characteristics of control MOSFET are appeared in Fig. 19 and Fig. 20.

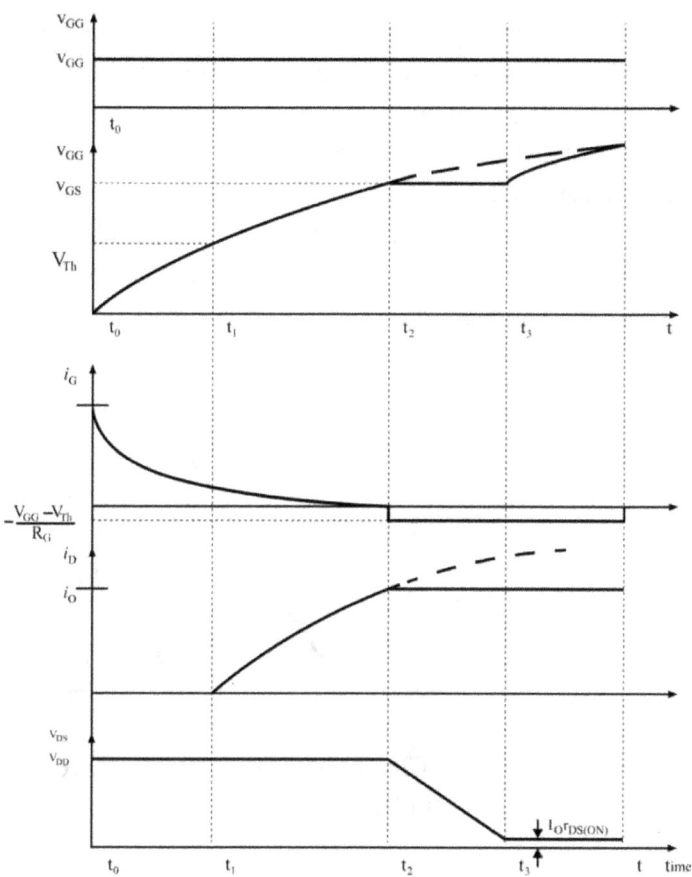

Figure 19. Turn-on Characteristics of Power MOSFET

There's a delay from t0 to t_1 due to charging of input capacitance up to its limit voltage V_{TH}. Deplete current in this length remains at zero value. This can be called a delay time. There's an assist delay from t_1 to t2 amid which the entryway voltage rises to V_{GS}, a voltage required to drive the MOSFET into on-state. This can be called the rise time.

This add up to delay can be diminished by employing a low-impedance drive circuit. The door current amid this term diminishes exponentially as appeared. For the time more prominent than t_2, the depletion layer current I_D has come to its greatest steady esteem I. As deplete current has come to the steady esteem, the gate-to-source voltage is additionally consistent as appeared within the exchange characteristics of MOSFET in Fig. 20.

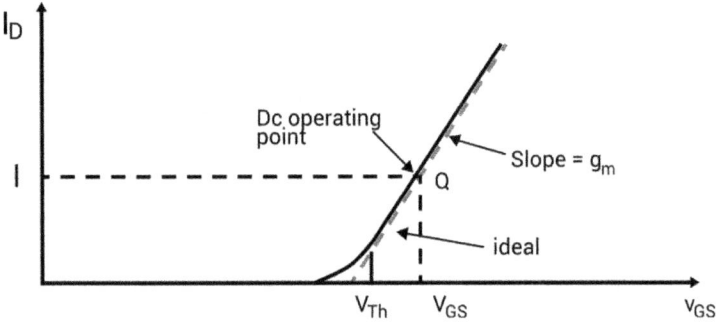

Figure 20. Transfer Characteristics of Power MOSFET with Operating Point

For turn-off characteristics, accept that the MOSFET is as of now within the switched-on circumstance with consistent state. As $t = t_0$, door voltage is decreased to zero esteem; C_{GS} and C_{GD} begin to release through door resistance R_G. This causes a turn-off delay time up to t1 from t0 as appeared in Fig. 21. Accepting the drain-to-source voltage remains settled. Amid this length, both V_{GS} and I_G diminishes in greatness, deplete current remains at a settled esteem drawing current from C_{GD} and C_{GS}.

For the time where $t_2 > t > t_1$, gate-to-source voltage is steady. Hence, the whole current is presently being drawn from CGD. Up to time t_3, the deplete current will nearly reach zero esteem; which turns off the MOSFET. This time is known as the drop time, this is often when the input capacitance releases up to the limit esteem. Past t_3, door voltage diminishes exponentially to zero until the door current gets to be zero.

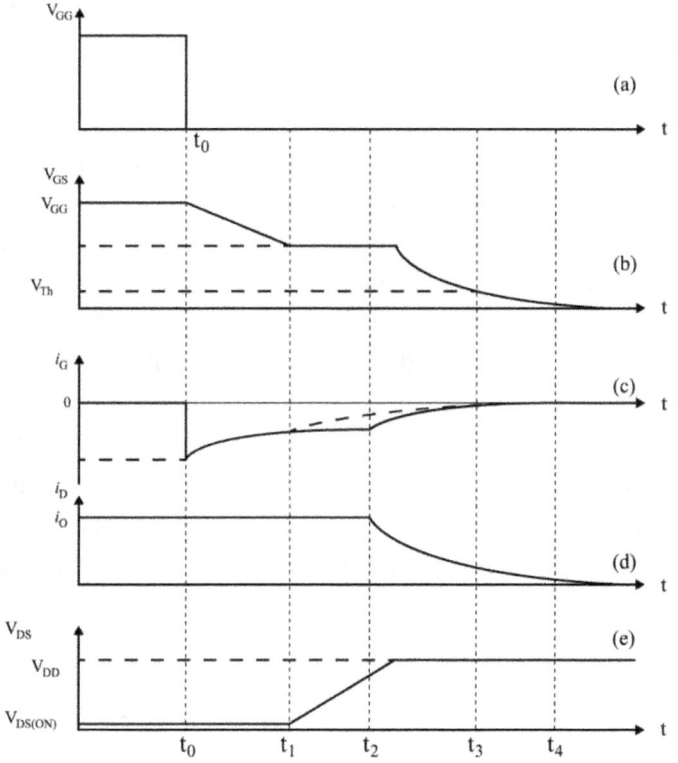

Figure 21. Turn-Off Characteristics of Power MOSFET

Power Bipolar Junction Transistor (BJT)

Control BJT is utilized customarily for numerous applications. Be that as it may, IGBT (Insulated-Gate Bipolar Transistor) and MOSFET (Metal-Oxide-Semiconductor Field-Effect Transistor) have supplanted it for most of the applications but still they are utilized in a few zones due to its lower immersion voltage over the working temperature extend. IGBT and MOSFET have higher input capacitance as compared to BJT. In this way, in case of IGBT and MOSFET, drive circuit must be able to charge and release the inner capacitances.

The BJT could be a three-layer and two-junction NPN or PNP semiconductor gadget as given in Fig. 22. (a) and (b). Although BJTs have lower input capacitance as compared to MOSFET or IGBT, BJTs are significantly slower in reaction due to moo input impedance. BJTs utilize more silicon for the same drive performance. In the case of MOSFET considered prior, control BJT is distinctive in setup as compared to basic planar BJT. In planar BJT, collector and emitter is on the same side of the wafer whereas in control BJT it is on the opposite edges as shown in Fig. 23. Usually done to extend the power-handling capability of BJT.

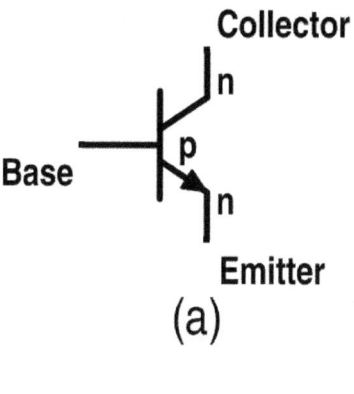

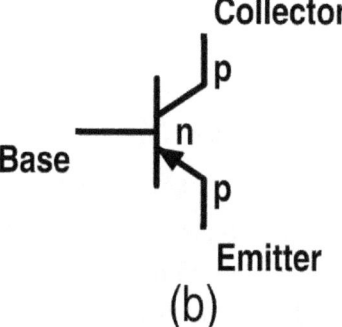

Figure 22. (a) NPN BJT (b) PNP BJT

Power n-p-n transistors are broadly utilized in high-voltage and high-current applications which is able be examined later

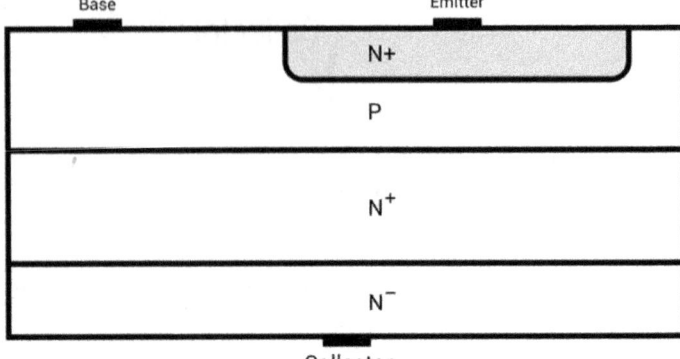

Figure 23. Power BJT PNP Structure

Input and yield characteristics of planar BJT for common-emitter setup are appeared in Fig. 24. These are current-voltage characteristics curves.

Characteristic bends for control BJT is fair the same but for the small distinction in its immersion locale. It has extra locale of operation known as quasi-saturation as appeared in Fig. 25.

This locale shows up due to the addition of lightly-doped collector float locale where the collector base intersection incorporates a moo turn around inclination.

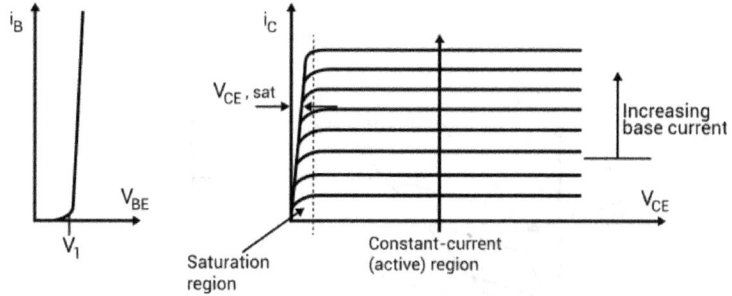

Figure 24. Input Characteristics and Output Characteristics for the Common-Emitter Configuration of Planar BJT respectively

The resistivity of this float locale is dependent on the esteem of the base current. Within the quasi-saturation locale, the esteem of ß diminishes essentially. Typically, due to the expanded esteem of the collector current with expanded temperature. But the base current still has the control over the collector current due to the resistance advertised by the float locale. In the event that the transistor enters in difficult immersion locale, base current has no control over the collector current due to the nonappearance of the float locale and primarily depends on the stack and the esteem of V_{CC}.

A forward-biased p-n intersection has two capacitances named consumption layer capacitance and diffused capacitance. Whereas an invert predisposition intersection has as it were a consumption capacitance in activity. Esteem of these capacitances depends on the intersection voltage and development of the transistor

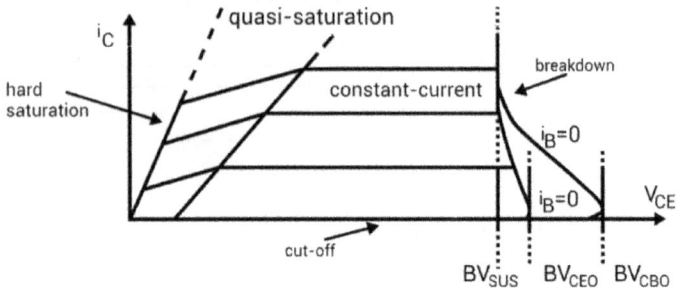

Figure 25. Power BJT Output Characteristics Curve

. These capacity these capacitances, transistor does not turn on or turn off immediately. Switching characteristics of control BJT is appeared in Fig.26. As the positive base voltage is connected, base current begins to stream but there's no collector current for a few time. This time is known as the delay time (t_d) required to charge the intersection capacitance of the base to emitter to 0.7 V approx. (known as forward-bias voltage). For $t > t_d$, collector current begins rising and V_{CE} begins to drop with the size of 9/10th of its crest esteem. This time is called rise time, required to turn on the transistor. The transistor remains on so long as the collector current is at slightest of this value. For turning off the BJT, extremity of the base voltage is turned around and in this way the base current extremity will too be changed as appeared in Fig. 26. The base current required amid the steady-state operation is more than that required to immerse the transistor. In this way, overabundance minority carrier charges are put away within the base reg

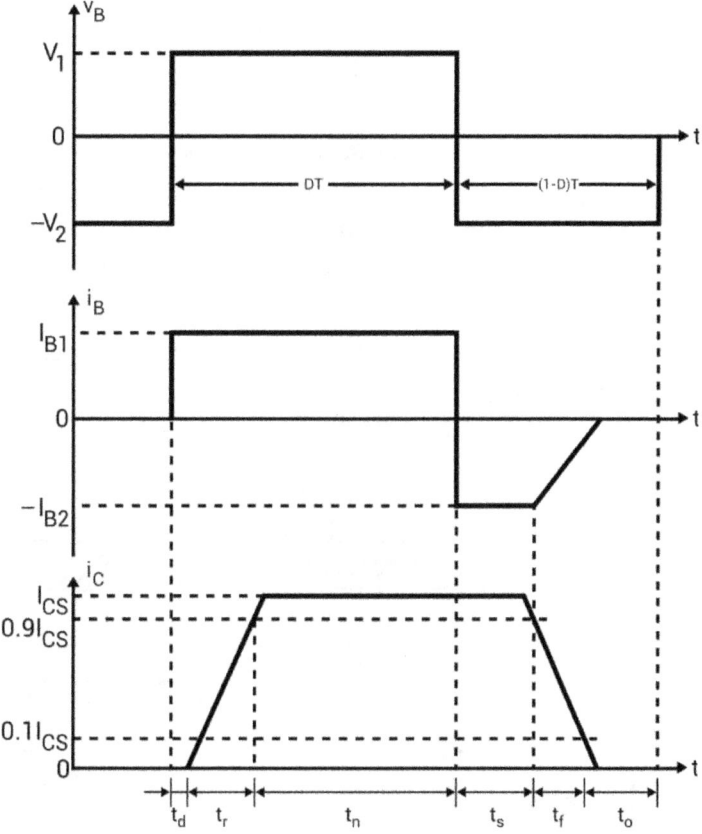

Figure 26. Turn-On and Turn-Off Characteristics of BJT

Insulated-Gate Bipolar Transistor (IGBT)

IGBT combines the material science of both BJT and control MOSFET to pick up the focal points of both universes. It is controlled by the door voltage. It has the tall input impedance like a control MOSFET and has moo on-state control misfortune as in case of BJT. There's no indeed auxiliary breakdown and not have long exchanging time as in case of BJT. It has way better conduction characteristics as compared to MOSFET due to bipolar nature. It has no body diode as in case of MOSFET but this may be seen as an advantage to utilize outside quick recuperation diode for particular applications. They are supplanting the MOSFET for most of the tall voltage applications with less conduction misfortunes. Its physical cross-sectional auxiliary graph and comparable circuit chart is displayed in Fig. 27 to Fig. 29. It has three terminals called collector, emitter and gate.

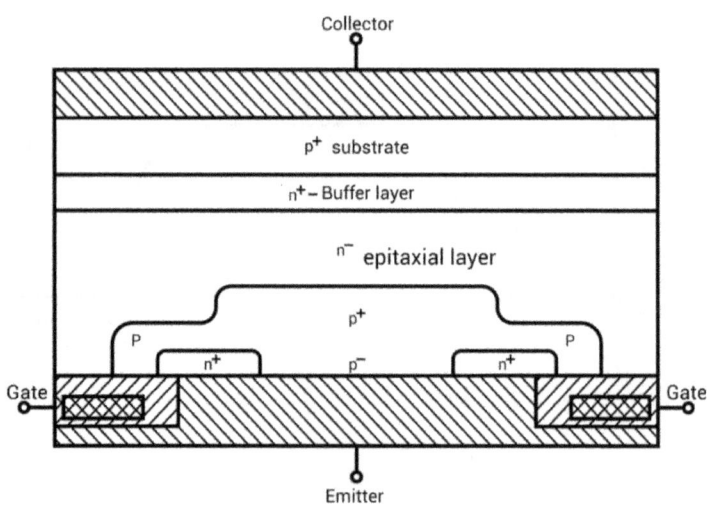

Figure 27. IGBT Structure View

There's a p+ substrate which isn't display within the MOSFET and dependable for the minority carrier infusion into the n-region. Pick up of NPN terminal is decreased due to wide epitaxial base and n+ buffer layer. There are two structures of IGBTs based on doping of buffer layer: a) Punch-through IGBT: Intensely doped n buffer layer ➔ less exchanging time b) Non-Punch-through IGBT: Softly doped n buffer layer ➔ more prominent carrier lifetime ➔ expanded conductivity of float locale ➔ diminished on-state voltage drop

(Note: ➔ means implies)

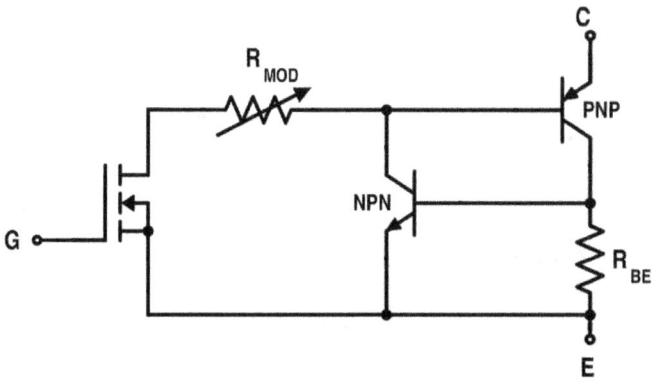

Figure 28. Equivalent Circuit for IGBT

Based on this circuit graph given in Fig.30, forward characteristics and exchange characteristics are gotten which are given in Fig.31 and Fig.32.

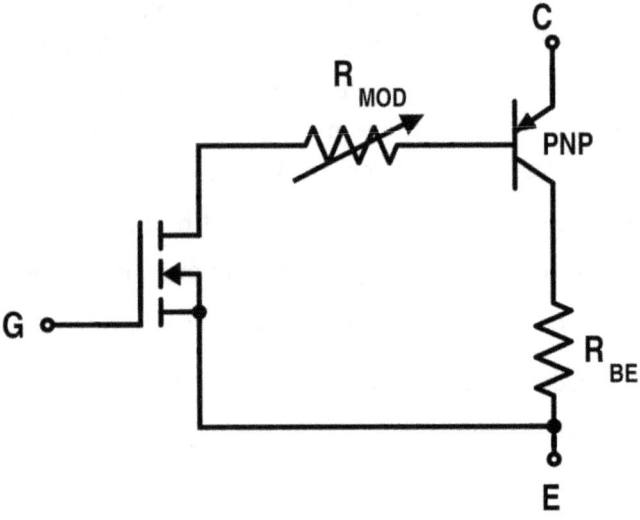

Figure 29. Simplified Equivalent Circuit for IGBT

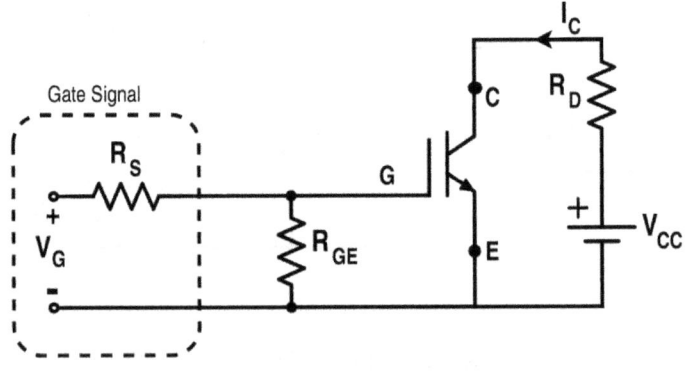

Figure 30. Circuit Diagram for IGBT

Its exchanging characteristic is additionally appeared in Fig. 33.

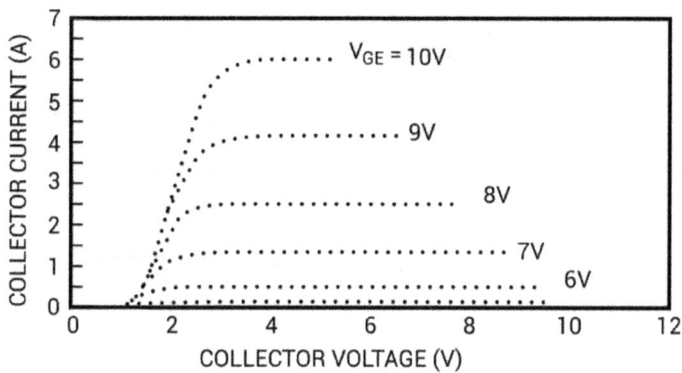

Figure 31. Forward Characteristics for IGBT

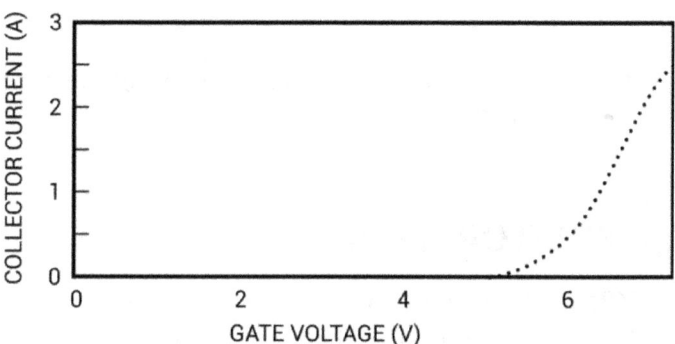

Figure 32. Transfer Characteristics of IGBT

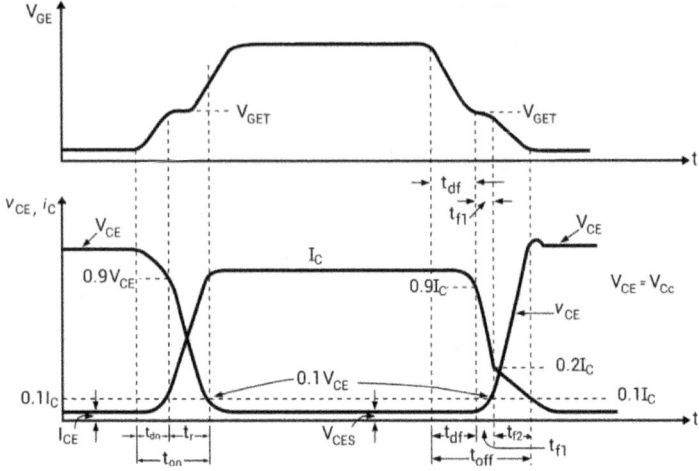

Figure 33. Turn-On and Turn-Off Characteristics of IGBT

(Note: T_{dn}: delay time; T_r: rise time; T_{df}: delay time; T_{f1}: initial fall time; T_{f2}: final fall time)

THYRISTORs (SCR, GTO, MCT)

THYRISTORs are the family of solid-state gadgets broadly utilized in control gadgets circuitry such as SCR (silicon-controlled rectifier), DIAC (diode on AC), TRIAC (triode on AC), GTO (entryway turn-off THYRISTORs), MCT (MOS-controlled THYRISTOR), RCT, PUT, UJT, LASCR, LASCS, SIT, SITh, SIS, SBS, SUS, SBS and etc. SCR is the most seasoned part and the head of this family; and ordinarily alluded with the title "THYRISTOR". They are worked as bistable switches that are either working in non-conducting or conducting state. Conventional THYRISTORs are planned without gate-controlled turn-off capability in which the THYRISTOR can come from conducting state to non-conducting state when as it were anode current falls underneath the holding current. Whereas GTO could be a sort of THYRISTOR that contains a gate-controlled turn-off capability.

SCR

SCR more often than not has three terminals and four layers of rotating p and n-type materials as appeared in Fig. 34. The structure of the THYRISTOR can be part into two segments: NPN and PNP transistors for straightforward examination purposes as appeared in Fig. 36. It has three terminals named as cathode, anode and door.

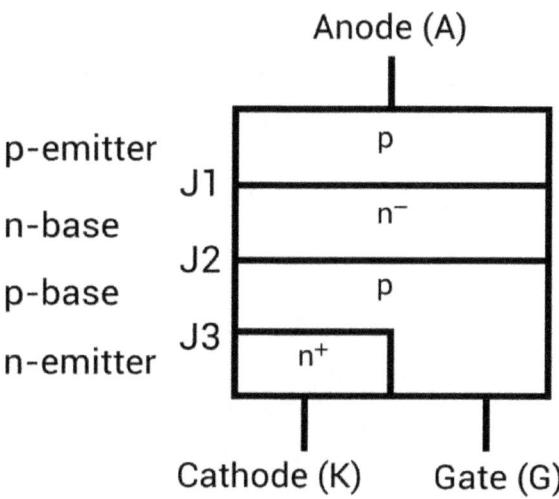

Figure 34. Structural View of THYRISTOR

N-base could be a high-resistivity locale and its thickness is straightforwardly subordinate on the forward blocking rating of the THYRISTOR. But more width of the n-base demonstrates a moderate reaction time for exchanging. Image of THYRISTOR is given in Fig. 35.

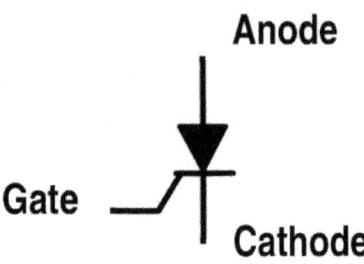

Figure 35. Schematic Symbol of THYRISTOR

Planar development is utilized for low-power SCRs. In this sort of development, all the intersections are diffused. For tall control, mesa development is utilized where the internal layer is diffused and the two external layers are alloyed on it.

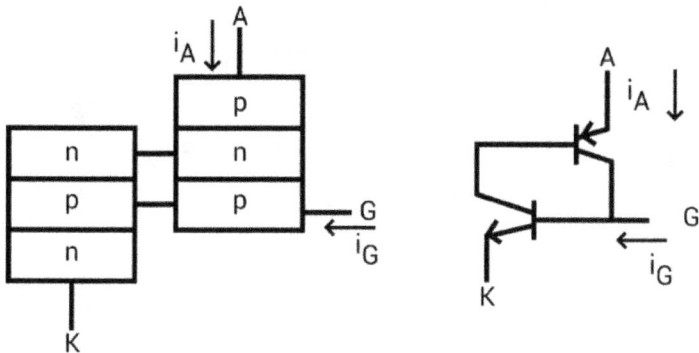

Figure 36. Two-Transistor Model of a THYRISTOR (A-Anode, G-Gate and K-Cathode)

The inactive characteristic gotten from the circuit given in Fig. 37 is drawn in Fig. 38. It works beneath three modes: forward conducting mode, forward blocking mode and invert blocking mode. The least anode current that causes the gadget to remain at forward conduction mode because it switches from forward blocking mode is called the hooking current. On the off chance that the SCR is as of now conducting and the anode current is decreased from forward conducting mode to forward blocking mode, the least esteem of anode current to stay at the forward conducting mode is known as the holding current.

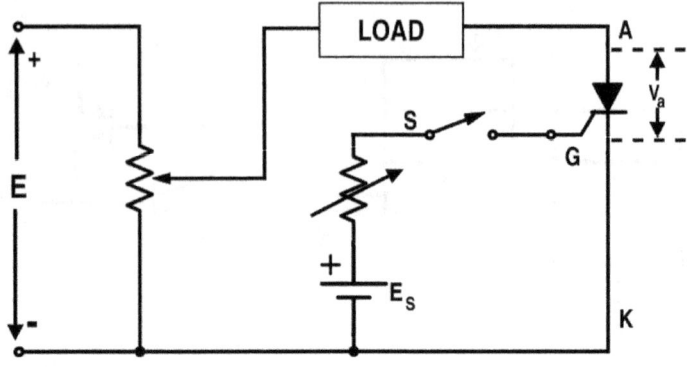

Figure 37. Basic Circuit for Getting Voltage and Current Characteristics of THYRISTOR

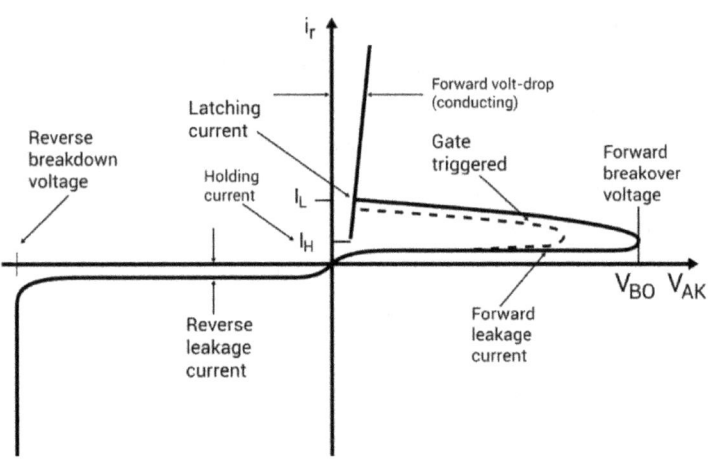

Figure 38. Static Characteristics Curve of SCR

Exchanging characteristics of SCR are appeared in Fig. 39. Note that it can't be turned off with the entryway.

Typically, due to positive criticism or a regenerative input impact.

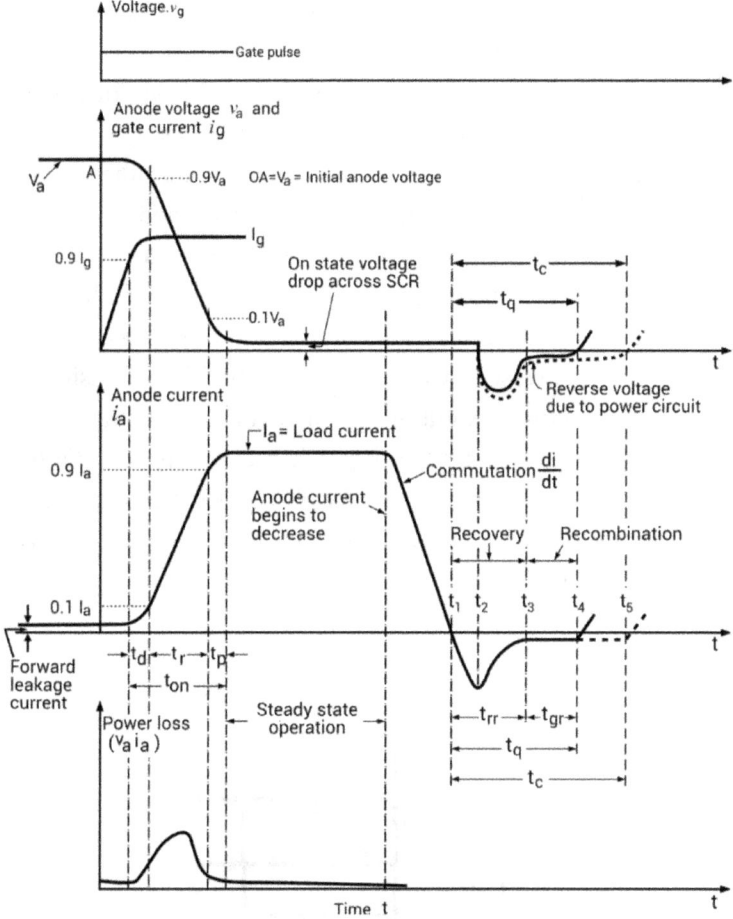

Figure 39. Turn-On and Turn-Off Characteristics of SCR

GTO (Gate Turn-off THYRISTOR)

GTO can be turned on with the positive entryway current beat and turned off with the negative door current beat. Its capability to turn off is due to the redirection of PNP collector current by the entryway and in this way breaking the regenerative input effect. Actually the plan of GTO is made in such a way that the PNP current pick up of GTO is decreased. Exceedingly doped n spots within the anode p layer frame a shorted emitter impact and eventually diminishes the current pick up of GTO for lower current recovery additionally the invert voltage blocking capability. This diminishment in invert blocking capability can be progressed by diffusing gold but this diminishes the carrier lifetime. Additionally, it requires an extraordinary assurance as appeared in Fig. 43. Fig. 40 appears the four Si layers and the three intersections of GTO and Fig. 41 appears it's down to earth shape. The image for GTO is appeared in Fig.42.

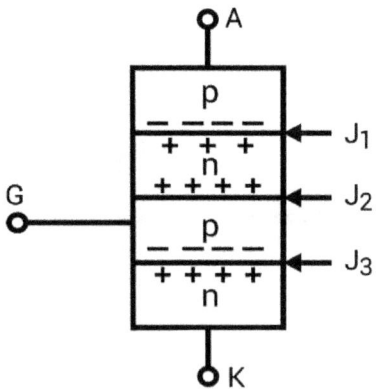

Figure 40. Four Layers and Three Junctions of GTO

By and large exchanging speed of GTO is speedier than THYRISTOR (SCR) but voltage drop of GTO is bigger. The control extend of GTO is way better than BJT, IGBT or SCR. The inactive voltage current characteristics of GTO are comparable to SCR but that the hooking current of GTO is bigger (almost 2 A) as compared to SCR (around 100-500 mA).

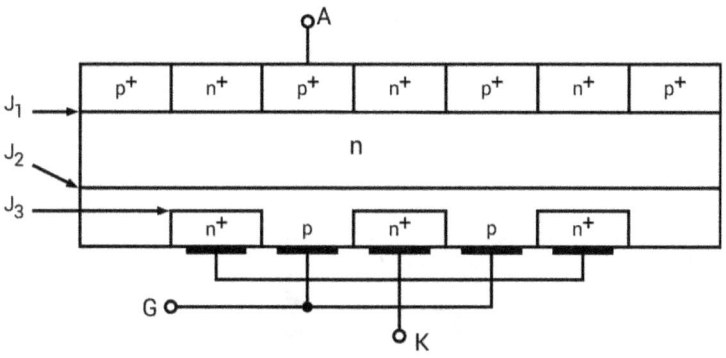

Figure 41. Practical Form of GTO

The entryway drive circuitry with exchanging characteristics is given in Fig. 43 and Fig. 44.

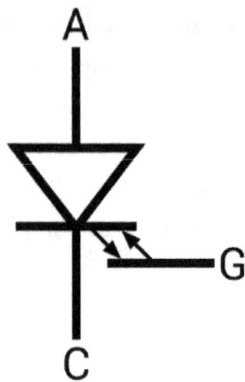

Figure 42. Symbol of GTO

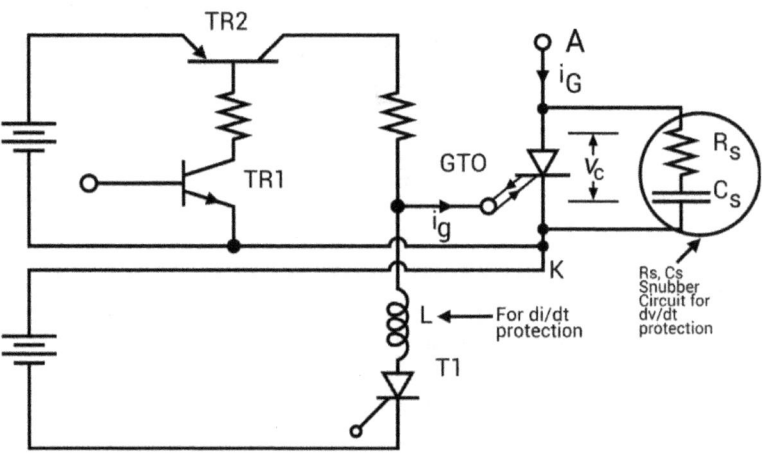

Figure 43. Gate Drive Circuit for GTO

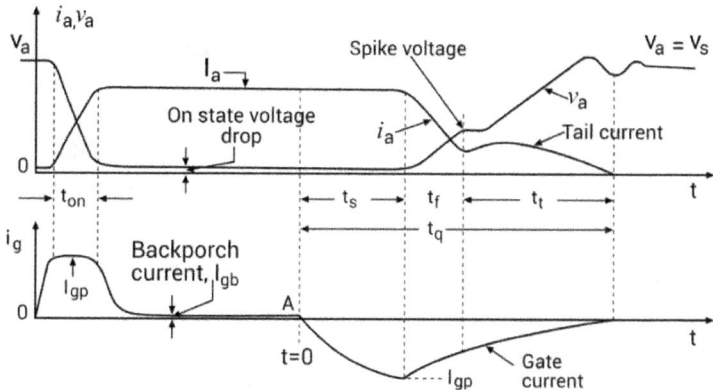

Figure 44. Turn-On and Turn-Off Characteristics of GTO

MCT (MOS-Controlled THYRISTOR)

IGBT is a change over a BJT employing a MOSFET to switch on or switch off the anode current. Additionally, MCT is a change over a THYRISTOR with a match of MOSFETs to switch the current.

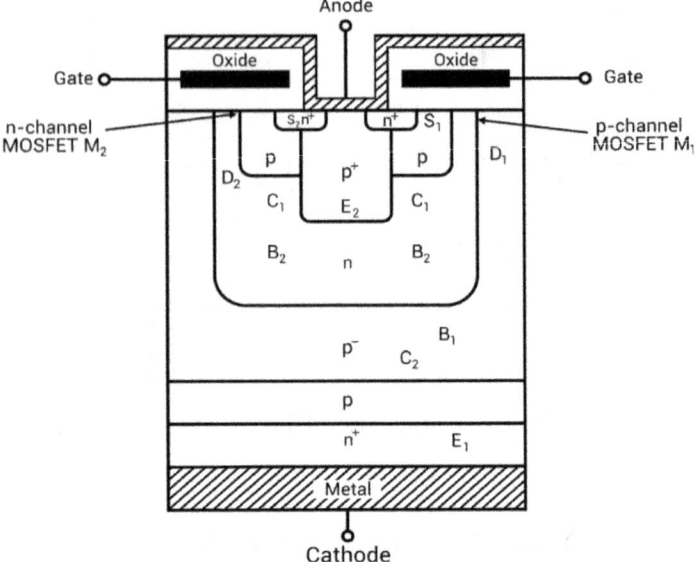

Figure 45. Schematic Diagram of P-Type MCT

There are a few gadgets within the MCT's family but the p-channel is commonly talked about. Its schematic chart and comparable circuit is given in Fig. 45 and Fig. 46. Its image is given in Fig. 47.

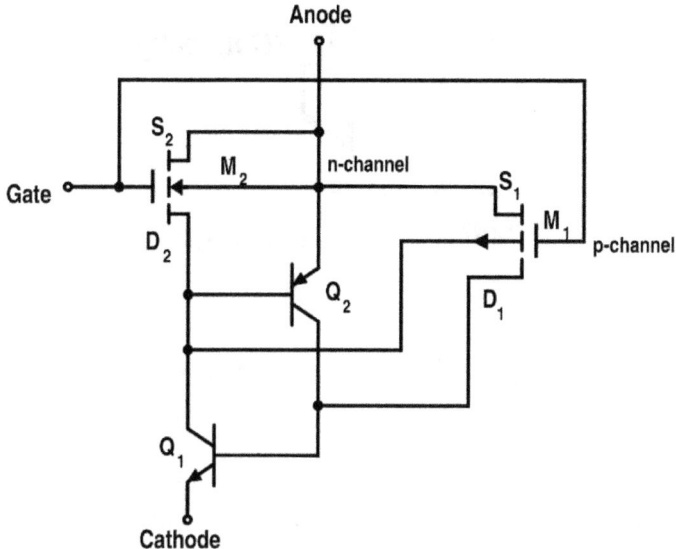

Figure 46. Equivalent Circuit for P-Type MCT

Due to NPNP structure rather than PNPN, anode acts as a reference for entryway. NPNP structure is spoken to by NPN transistor Q1 and a PNP transistor Q2 within the identical circuit. The control required to switch it on or off is little with moo switching losses due to its dispersed structure over the complete surface of the device.

Delay time due to charge capacity is additionally little. It too features a moo on-state voltage drop. When a p-type MCT is within the forward-blocking state, it can be exchanged on by applying a negative beat to its entryway (with regard to anode).

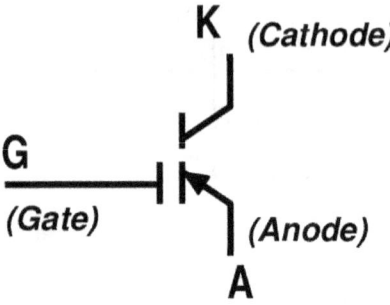

Figure 47. Symbol of P-Type MCT

Whereas when an n-channel MCT is within the forward-blocking mode, it can be exchanged on with the positive entryway beat (with regard to cathode). It'll stay on until the gadget current is turned around or a turn-off beat is connected to the door i.e. applying a positive door beat for p-type MCT with regard to anode.

This gadget can bear a tall current and tall di/dt, di/dt capability. But rather like any other gadgets, it ought to be secured against transitory voltages and current spikes with the assistance of reasonable snubbers. It is utilized in capacitor discharge applications, circuit breakers, AC-AC or AC-DC transformation. It is a perfect substitution for GTO because it requires a much less complex entryway drive and certainly more effective

References

1- Power Electronic Converters: Dynamics and Control in Conventional and Renewable Energy Applications, Teuvo Suntio, Tuomas Messo, et al, 2017, ISBN: 978-3527340224

2- Introduction to Power Electronics (Essential Electronics), D. Fewson, 1998, ISBN: 978-0340691434

3- Power Electronics: Principles of Analysis and Design with Emphasis on Magnetics Volume 1, Thomas G. Wilson, et al, 2019, ISBN: 978-1543140613

4- Analysis and Design of Power Converter Topologies for Application in Future More Electric Aircraft (Springer Theses) , Amit Kumar Singh, 2018, ISBN: 978-9811082122

www.ingramcontent.com/pod-product-compliance
Lightning Source LLC
Chambersburg PA
CBHW072035060426
42449CB00010BA/2276